amazing party cakes

amazing party cakes

50 fun and fantasy cakes for kids

southwater

This edition is published by Southwater

Distributed in the UK by
The Manning Partnership
251–253 London Road East
Batheaston
Bath BA1 7RL
tel. 01225 852 727
fax 01225 852 852

Published in the USA by
Anness Publishing Inc.
27 West 20th Street
Suite 504
New York
NY 10011
fax 212 807 6813

Distributed in Canada by
General Publishing
895 Don Mills Road
400–402 Park Centre
Toronto, Ontario M3C 1W3
tel. 416 445 3333
fax 416 445 5991

Distributed in Australia by
Sandstone Publishing
Unit 1, 360 Norton Street
Leichhardt
New South Wales 2040
tel. 02 9560 7888
fax 02 9560 7488

Southwater is an imprint of Anness Publishing Limited
Hermes House, 88–89 Blackfriars Road, London SE1 8HA
tel. 020 7401 2077; fax 020 7633 9499

© 1994, 1995, 2001 Anness Publishing Limited

Publisher: Joanna Lorenz
Senior Editor: Lindsay Porter
Editor: Gillian Haslam
Designer: Peter Laws
Jacket design: The Bridgewater Book Company Ltd
Photographer: Edward Allwright
Assistant Home Economist: Lucy McKelvie
Stylist: Maria Kelly
Production Controller: Joanna King

Previously published as *Step-by-Step: 50 Children's Party Cakes*

1 3 5 7 9 10 8 6 4 2

NOTES

Standard spoon and cup measures are level.
Large eggs are used unless otherwise stated.

CONTENTS

Introduction	6
ANIMAL CAKES	18
FANTASY CAKES	34
FUN AND GAMES	48
TRANSPORTATION	72
CAKES FOR ALL OCCASIONS	80
TEMPLATES	92
Index	96

INTRODUCTION

A novelty cake is the perfect way to celebrate a child's birthday or other special event, and can form the focal point of a particular party theme. All of the cakes in this book are based on square or round sponge cakes, and many are ideal for busy parents, who want to create something special but don't have the time or experience to produce labour-intensive icing effects. Many of the designs are quite simple, and are enhanced with colorful candies and small decorations — the children will love the additional sweets, and can save the decorations as mementos of their special day. The cakes can also be made a few days ahead of the party, and as long as they are covered with fondant and stored in a cool place, they can be worked on gradually, whenever you are able to find the time.

Of the 50 cake decorating ideas — from pirate hats to fairy castles — there will be something to appeal to children of all ages — and you won't have to spend precious hours in the kitchen to achieve fantastic results. Delight friends and family with a glorious cake and make every children's party an instant success!

Equipment

Cake boards
Silver cake boards are perfect for presenting finished cakes. They come in a variety of shapes and sizes, in circles, squares and rectangles from 4 in to 12 in in diameter.

Cake pans
All the cakes in this book use round or square pans in a variety of sizes. 6 in, 8 in and 10 in are the most useful.

Electric hand-held beaters
These are real time-savers when making up cake batters and icings.

Icing smoother
This will give a wonderfully uniform finish to fondant-covered cakes.

Measuring spoons
These are available in both metric and imperial measurements. Always measure level unless otherwise stated.

Mixing bowls
A set of various sizes is useful for mixing cake batters and icings.

Spatulas
These are useful for spreading butter cream onto cakes.

Pastry brush
This is essential for greasing cake pans, and brushing cakes with apricot glaze.

Plastic chopping board
Use this as a smooth, flat surface to roll fondant if you do not have a Formica work surface.

Plastic scrapers
These can be used to create all sorts of 'combed' patterns in butter cream.

Rolling pin
Use a heavy rolling pin for rolling out marzipan and fondant.

Round pastry cutters
A set of cutters in various sizes can be used to create perfect rounds of fondant for decoration.

Sable paint brushes
These are expensive, but are well worth the extra cost when painting fine details onto cakes.

Serrated knives
Sharp knives with a serrated edge will allow you to cut cakes without breaking.

Sieves
Larger sieves are used for sifting flour into cake batter, and confectioners' sugar into icing to prevent lumps. Smaller ones are used to sift confectioners' sugar onto a work top when rolling out fondant.

Turntable
This enables you to turn the cake as you decorate which makes the task simpler.

Weighing scales
These are essential for accuracy when weighing ingredients for cakes.

Wooden toothpicks
These can be used to make designs on cakes, or to support pieces of cake to make a particular shape. If toothpicks are used as support, *always* remove them before serving.

Wooden spoons
A selection of wooden spoons is useful for stirring batters and icings.

weighing scales

cake p

serrated knives

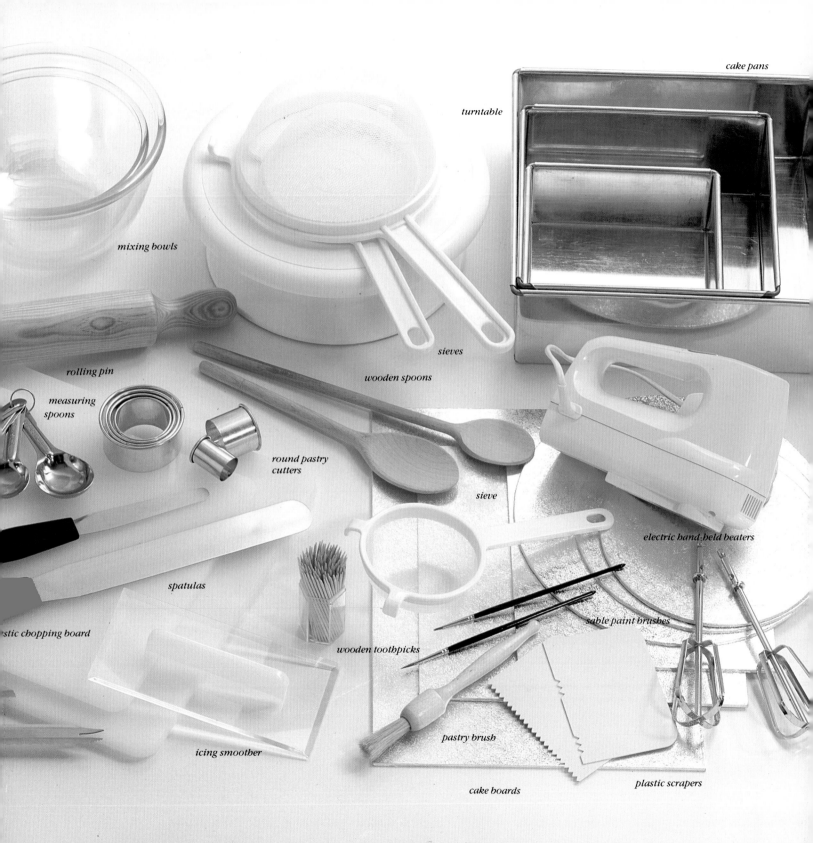

cake pans

turntable

mixing bowls

sieves

rolling pin

wooden spoons

measuring
spoons

round pastry
cutters

sieve

electric hand-held beaters

spatulas

sable paint brushes

stic chopping board

wooden toothpicks

icing smoother

pastry brush

cake boards

plastic scrapers

Cake Decorations

Specialist cake decorating shops will stock a variety of inexpensive, appealing items that can be used to enhance cakes.

edible paste colors

numbers

flower cutters and ejecters

powder blossom tints

metal piping tubes

plastic train set

mini ribbon bows

novelties and toys

candles

sugar mouse

candle holders

cutters

Candles
A wide variety of shapes and colors are available from cake decorating shops and large department stores.

Candle holders
These are made of plastic, and come in various colors and sizes. They are available from both specialist suppliers and party shops.

Cutters
The varieties shown include a daisy flower cutter, a holly leaf cutter and a small flower cutter. They can be used for cutting fondant into specific shapes for decoration. These metal cutters can be purchased from specialist cake decorating shops and kitchenware suppliers.

Edible paste colors
These are very concentrated, so use sparingly. They can be kneaded thoroughly into fondants to produce a uniform color.

Left: *A range of delightful items used to enhance cakes. Specialist shops will carry a variety of items, but toy shops will also carry small toys and novelties.*

Flower cutters with ejecters

These can be bought singly or in a boxed set with a small round sponge, and come in ¼ in, ⅜ in and ½ in sizes. The ejector is on a spring, and the icing flowers are pressed out of the cutter on to the sponge, to both shape and mold them simultaneously.

Metal piping tubes

These are expensive but it is worth investing in the best quality as they will produce lovely icing effects and will last for years. The most useful ones to buy initially to start your collection are the no. 22 basket weave tube (a flat tube with a serrated edge); no. 1 writing tube (for writing, drawing outlines and producing run-outs); nos. 7 and 8 star tubes and no. 44 scroll tube for piping borders.

Mini ribbon bows

These are delightful additions to cakes and are bought in packs of 12, in all sorts of colors. Simply stick them into icing.

Novelties and toys

You are likely to find a novelty to reflect almost any theme you wish in the better cake decorating shops. Illustrated here are plastic treble clefs, plastic miniature aeroplanes and plastic silver bells. The wooden sailing boat was purchased from a toy shop, another good source of small toys and novelties.

Plastic train set

This has the advantage of also holding candles. The carriages are detachable so the correct number of candles may be used.

Powder blossom tints

These are edible dusting powders which come in various colors, and are used for brushing onto fondant icing to produce subtle shading. They can also be mixed to a paste with a product called rejuvenator, and then painted directly onto fondant like paints. Both products are available from specialist cake decorating shops.

Sugar mice

This example is home-made, and was made in a plastic mold with a string tail, but sugar animals can also be purchased from specialist confectioners.

Lining a Cake Pan

Lining pans is important so that the cakes come out of the pan without breaking or sticking to the base of the pan. This method is simple, but essential.

1 Place the pan on a piece of waxed paper, draw around the base with a pencil and cut out the paper inside this line.

2 Grease the base and sides of the pan with melted lard or soft margarine and stick the piece of paper in neatly. Grease the paper. It is now ready for filling.

Apricot Glaze

This is used to seal the cake and stop the crumbs working their way into the icing. It will also stick the marzipan or fondant to the cake.

INGREDIENTS
½ cup apricot jam
1 tbsp water

1 Heat the apricot jam in a pan with the water, then rub through a sieve to remove any lumps. Return to the pan and heat until boiling before brushing carefully over the cake.

Basic Recipes

The recipes in this book all use simple round or square cake shapes. Make up the cake to the required size, according to the chart on these pages.

For the lightest sponge cakes, use polyunsaturated margarine. Margarine can be used straight from the fridge so all the ingredients can be put in a bowl and whisked together as there is no need to cream the fat and sugar first.

To make up the required amounts of butter cream, use the amount of confectioners' sugar specified for the total weight of frosting (ie 2¾ cups butter cream requires 2¾ cups confectioners' sugar). Consult the chart to establish the proportions of butter and milk required per amount of confectioners' sugar.

Where a recipe calls for fondant or marzipan, you can use the store-bought variety to save time, or make your own. For fondant, calculate the proportions as above (total weight of fondant required is equal to the amount of sugar used). The marzipan recipe may be made in larger or smaller quantities as required. The royal icing recipe can also be made in smaller or larger batches, with the sugar used equal to the total weight called for in the recipe.

BASIC SPONGE CAKE AND BUTTERCREAM

6 in round cake:
2 eggs
½ cup superfine sugar
½ cup butter or margarine
1 cup self-rising flour
½ tsp baking powder
1 tbsp water

Butter cream:
1 tbsp butter
1½ tsp milk
½ cup confectioners' sugar, sifted

Baking time:
35–45 minutes

8 in round cake
3 eggs
¾ cup superfine sugar
¾ cup butter or margarine
1½ cups self-rising flour
¾ tsp baking powder
2 tbsp water

Butter cream:
2 tbsp butter
1 tbsp milk
1 cup confectioners' sugar, sifted

Baking time:
45–55 minutes

10 in round cake
6 eggs
1½ cups superfine sugar
1½ cups butter or margarine
3 cups self-rising flour
1½ tsp baking powder
5 tbsp water

Butter cream:
¼ cup butter
2 tbsp milk
1½ cups confectioners' sugar, sifted

Baking time:
1–1¼ hours

6 in square cake:
3 eggs
¾ cup superfine sugar
½ cup butter or margarine
1½ cups self-rising flour
¾ tsp baking powder
2 tbsp water

Butter cream:
1 tbsp butter
1½ tsp milk
½ cup confectioners' sugar, sifted

Baking time:
45–55 minutes

8 in square cake
4 eggs
1 cup superfine sugar
1 cup butter or margarine
2 cups self-rising flour
1 tsp baking powder
3 tbsp water

Butter cream:
2 tbsp butter
1 tbsp milk
1 cup confectioners' sugar, sifted

Baking time:
50–60 minutes

10 in square cake
8 eggs
2 cups superfine sugar
2 cups butter or margarine
4 cups self-rising flour
2 tsp baking powder
7 tbsp water

Butter cream:
¼ cup butter
2 tbsp milk
1½ cups confectioners' sugar, sifted

Baking time:
1½–1¾ hours

Basic Sponge Cake

All the cakes in this book are based on basic sponge cakes. Consult the chart for the correct proportions needed, and follow the simple steps below.

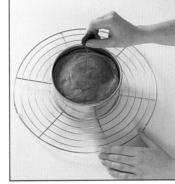

1 Preheat the oven to 375°F. To grease and base line the cake pans, trace around the base of the tin you will be using on waxed paper and cut out the circle. Grease the inside of the tin lightly with melted lard or margarine, then press the waxed paper onto the bottom of the pan.

2 Place the eggs, sugar, margarine and flour into a large bowl. Measure the baking powder level and add.

5 Bake in the center of the oven for about 25 minutes to 1 hour for the largest size, or until a thin skewer inserted into the center of the cake comes out clean. Loosen the sides carefully with a knife. Cover a wire cooling rack with a piece of waxed paper (this will prevent the cake from sticking) and turn the cake onto the rack. Cool completely.

3 Whisk all the ingredients together until light and fluffy.

4 Spoon into the prepared pan. Spread evenly to the sides.

TO MAKE BUTTER CREAM

Soften the butter, add the milk and whisk in the sifted confectioners' sugar until smooth. Add any flavoring and coloring.

Marzipan

All the cakes are covered with a layer of marzipan. It seals in the moisture and gives a smooth, flat surface on which to ice. It is easy to work with and useful for modeling. If your children do not like marzipan, then replace with a layer of fondant.

INGREDIENTS
2 cups ground almonds
1 ¼ cups superfine sugar
1 ¼ cups confectioners' sugar, sifted
1 egg
1–2 tbsp lemon juice
¼ tsp almond extract

1 Mix all the dry ingredients in a bowl. Whisk the egg with the lemon juice and almond extract and add this to the almond and sugars in the bowl.

2 Mix thoroughly to form a pliable paste. Wrap in platic wrap until needed. Roll out on a work surface dusted with a little sifted confectioners' sugar.

Royal Icing

This is used for piping, run-outs and sticking decorations onto cakes. It dries very hard and holds its shape when piped.

INGREDIENTS
1 large egg white
1 ½ cups confectioners' sugar, sifted

COOK'S TIP

Dried egg white powder is available from supermarkets. It is whisked together with water and sifted confectioners' sugar, following the instructions on the package. It, too, must be covered at all times, as it dries very quickly.

1 Whisk the egg white in a large bowl with a fork. Add a quarter of the confectioners' sugar and beat well.

2 Gradually work in the remaining confectioners' sugar, beating well between each addition until the mixture holds its shape. Lay a piece of plastic wrap on top of the icing and cover the bowl with a damp cloth to prevent the icing drying out. Store at room temperature.

Quick Fondant Icing

This can be bought or home-made. It is soft and pliable
and must be worked with fairly quickly, as it will dry
out. It should be wrapped securely in plastic wrap if
you are not using it. Roll out on a smooth work surface
dusted with a little sifted confectioners' sugar or
cornstarch. It remains fairly soft for cutting and eating.

INGREDIENTS
3¼ cups confectioners' sugar, sifted
1 large egg white
2 tbsp liquid glucose
cornstarch

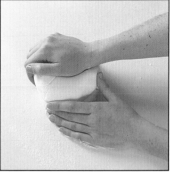

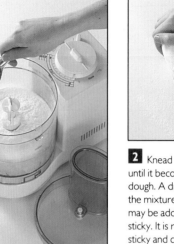

1 Put the confectioners' sugar, egg
white and glucose into a food processor
or mixer and blend together until the
mixture resembles fine breadcrumbs.

2 Knead the mixture with your hands
until it becomes smooth and pliable, like
dough. A drop of water may be added if
the mixture is too dry. A little cornstarch
may be added to prevent it becoming
sticky. It is ready when it no longer feels
sticky and can be rolled out. (The whole
process can be done by hand in a bowl.)

Gelatin Fondant Icing

This type of fondant icing is used for fine molding
decorations as it dries very hard.

INGREDIENTS
4 tbsp water
½ oz unflavored gelatin
2 tsp liquid glucose
3¼ cups confectioners' sugar, sifted
cornstarch

1 Put the water in a heatproof bowl
and sprinkle on the gelatin. Soak for 2
minutes. Place the bowl in a pan of hot
but not boiling water, stir until the gelatin
has dissolved and becomes clear. Remove
from the pan and stir in the liquid glucose,
then stir to cool slightly.

2 Put the sifted confectioners' sugar
into a bowl and mix in the gelatin mixture.
Add more sugar or cornstarch if the
mixture is too wet, or a little water if it is
too dry. Knead until smooth and pliable,
wrap in plastic wrap until needed.

COLORING FONDANT

Specialist cake decorating shops sell a
wide range of colors. Only the thick
paste colors must be used to color the
fondant, as liquid colors will make it
too wet. Simply knead in thoroughly
to the ready-made fondant. Colored
lustre powders are available to brush
on after the icing has dried. Different
effects can be achieved by applying
the colors not only with a soft brush
but on a sponge. A pale wash of color
can be painted on the icing and
allowed to dry, then a fairly dry brush
can be dragged across to give a
'woodgrain' effect.

Making a Waxed Paper Piping Bag

Piping bags for icing are simple to make at home. Make one for each coloring you will need.

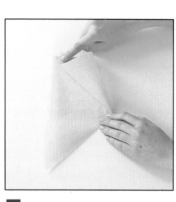

1 Cut waxed paper into 10 in square. Fold in half diagonally to make a triangle. Fold again to mark the center of the folded edge.

2 Then, holding the center, roll one point of the triangle up to the central line and the other point around that to make a tight cone.

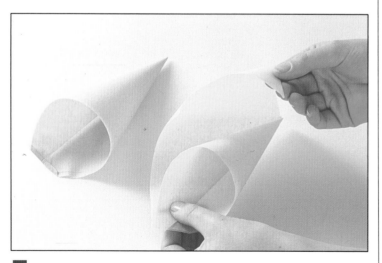

3 Fold the edges over to secure the top of the bag.

Using a Piping Bag

Using a piping bag takes a little practice initially. It's best to try a few sample designs first.

1 Cut off the tip, insert a piping tube and half-fill with royal icing.

2 Push the icing down well and fold both corners of the bag over to secure. Fold the top edge down several times until the icing is tightly packed in the bag.

3 Hold the bag in one hand and pipe in an upright position, guiding the bag with the other hand.

Making Run-outs

Run-outs can be piped onto the cake or onto a piece of waxed paper which has been secured with masking tape to ensure that there are no creases. Draw the shapes onto the paper then pipe the outlines, which can then be flooded to fill the center with a smooth, slightly domed surface. Always use freshly made icing.

1 Pipe the outline with No. 1 writing tube, following the marks on the waxed paper. Then thin the icing with a drop of water. Be careful not to make the icing too runny or it will overflow the sides and if it is too thick, it will not give a smooth surface. The correct consistency of the icing for 'flooding' should collapse and lose its shape if the bowl is tapped.

2 Half-fill a waxed piping bag with soft icing, snip off a small hole and fill the outline shape generously to make the surface slightly domed. Use a pin to coax the icing into difficult areas and to break any bubbles as soon as they appear on the surface.

3 Allow the run-outs to dry for at least 48 hours before peeling away the paper. Stick on the cake with a little royal icing.

Making and Using Templates

Templates are a useful way of transferring a design from a book or drawing onto the surface of a cake. There are some designs, letters and numbers at the back of the book to use.

1 Place tracing or waxed paper over the design to be copied and, using a sharp pencil, outline it neatly. If tracing a name, first draw a straight line on the paper with a ruler so that all the letters are even.

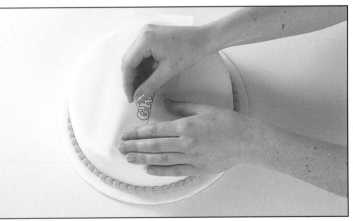

2 Turn the paper over and outline the design on the underside with a pencil. Turn the tracing the right way up and outline again onto the cake. A faint pencil outline will transfer onto the cake. A more laborious method is pricking the design through the paper straight onto the cake with a pin.

3 Now the design can be piped over the outline to cover any marks.

Cat in a Basket

The pretty woven pattern of the basket is quite simple to do but is surprisingly realistic. If you cannot model a cat from marzipan then use a suitable ornament.

INGREDIENTS
6 in round cake
¼ cup butter cream
2¼ cups pink marzipan
1½ cups green marzipan
1½ cups yellow marzipan
¼ cup white fondant
apricot glaze
food colorings: red, green, yellow and
  brown

EQUIPMENT
8 in round cake board
fine paint brush

apricot glaze

marzipan

fondant

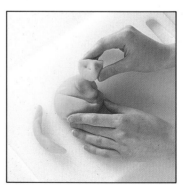

1 Split and fill the cake with butter cream. Place on the cake board. Measure the circumference of the cake with string, fold in half and measure (this will give the length of the marzipan strips to be cut). Brush with hot apricot glaze.

2 Roll out the pink marzipan to a 14 × 18 in rectangle. Cut into five ½ in strips, long enough to fit half way round the cake, about 10 in. Cut the green marzipan into 3 in lengths of the same width. Fold back alternate pink strips and lay a green strip across widthwise. Fold back the pink strips over the green strip to form the weave, fold back the second lot of pink strips and repeat the process. Press lightly to join.

3 Press the basket weave onto sides of cake, joining the sides neatly.

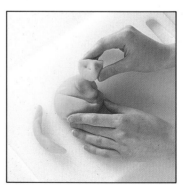

4 Model a yellow cat about 3 in across. Leave to dry overnight.

5 Roll out the fondant and place onto the cake and arrange in folds around the cat. Trim the edges.

6 Roll out any leftover pink and green marzipan into long ropes. Twist together and lay around the edge of the basket then press on neatly. With a fine paint brush and brown coloring, paint the face and markings on the cat.

Bella Bunny

This is a simple cake for very young children. The icing is spread over the cake and does not require any special techniques.

INGREDIENTS
6 in round cakes
2¼ cups butter cream
apricot glaze
2 cups shredded coconut
¼ cup white fondant
food colorings: red and brown
marshmallows

EQUIPMENT
10 × 14 in cake board
6 wooden toothpicks, stained brown
    with food coloring
candles

butter cream

apricot glaze

shredded coconut

marshmallows

I Split and fill the cakes with a little butter cream. Cut a 4 in circle out of one cake and place both cakes on the cake board. Round off any sharp edges.

2 Use the trimmings to make the ears and feet.

3 Brush with hot apricot glaze. Cover with the remaining butter cream then cover with coconut, pressing on lightly. Color a piece of fondant pink and roll and shape the nose. Cut out oval shapes for the ears and put into place. Color a small piece of fondant brown, roll two small balls for the eyes and put into place with the nose. Stick toothpicks on either side of nose for whiskers. Push the candles into the marshmallows and place on the board around the cake.

Pink Monkey

This cheeky little monkey can be made in any color fondant you wish.

INGREDIENTS
8 in round cake
¾ cup butter cream
apricot glaze
3 cups marzipan
3 cups pink fondant
¼ cup white fondant
food colorings: pink, blue and black

EQUIPMENT
10 in round cake board
candles

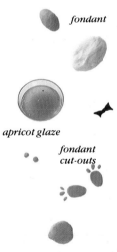

fondant

apricot glaze

fondant cut-outs

fondant

1 Split and fill the cake with butter cream. Place on the cake board and with a sharp serrated knife, use the template to cut out the basic shape of the monkey. Use the trimmings to shape the nose and tummy. Brush with hot apricot glaze and cover with a layer of marzipan then pink fondant. Leave to dry overnight.

2 Mark the position of the paws and face. Color a little of the fondant blue, roll out and cut out the eyes. Color a little fondant black and cut out the pupils and tie.

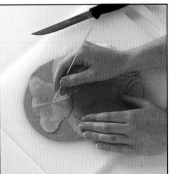

3 Color the remaining fondant pink and cut out the paws, nose, mouth and ears. Stick the features in place with water. Roll the trimmings into two balls and place on the board for the candles.

Mouse in Bed

This cake is suitable for almost any age. The duvet and sheets may reflect the child's favorite color. Make the mouse well ahead to allow it time to dry.

INGREDIENTS
8 in square cake
¾ cup butter cream
apricot glaze
3 cups marzipan
3 cups fondant
food colorings: blue and pink

EQUIPMENT
10 in square cake board
edible food color pens: pink and blue
flower cutter

white fondant

marzipan

fondant

I Split and fill the cake with butter cream. Cut 2 in off one side and reserve; the cake should measure 8 × 6 in. Place on the cake board and brush with hot apricot glaze. Cover with a layer of marzipan. With the reserved cake, cut a pillow to fit the bed and cover with marzipan, pressing a hollow in the middle for the head. Cut a mound for the body and legs of the mouse and cover with marzipan. Leave to dry overnight.

2 Cover the cake and pillow with white fondant. Lightly press a fork around the edge to make a frill around the pillow. Roll out 2¼ cups of fondant and cut into 3 in wide strips. Wet around the edge of the bed and drape the valance around.

3 To make the top sheet and quilt; color ½ cup of fondant blue and roll out to a 7 in square to cover the bed. Lightly mark a diamond pattern with the back of a knife and press a flower cutter into the diamonds to mark. Put the pillow and body on top of the cake and cover with the quilt.

4 Roll out a little white fondant and cut a 1 × 7½ in strip for the sheet, mark along one length to resemble a seam and place over the quilt, tucking it in at the top.

5 Color 2 tbsp of marzipan pink and make the head and paws of the mouse.

6 Put the mouse into bed with the paws over the edge of the sheet. Draw facial markings onto the mouse with edible food color pens.

Spider's Web

Make the marzipan spider several days before you need the cake to allow it time to dry. It is important to get the consistency of the glacé icing right; you can practise by pouring the icing onto a baking tray and piping on the web.

INGREDIENTS
8 in round cake
1½ cups butter cream
apricot glaze
1 tbsp cocoa powder
chocolate vermicelli
4 tbsp yellow marzipan
food colorings: red and brown
1½ cups confectioners' sugar
1–2 tbsp water

EQUIPMENT
10 in round cake board
wooden toothpick
star tube
candles

butter cream

apricot glaze

marzipan

chocolate vermicelli

1 Split and fill the cake with half the butter cream. Brush the sides with hot apricot glaze. Add the cocoa to the remaining butter cream then smooth a little over the sides of the cake. Roll the sides of the cake in the chocolate vermicelli and place on the cake board.

2 To make the spider, roll 2 tbsp of the yellow marzipan into two balls for the body and thorax. Color a small piece of marzipan red and roll into small dots, then stick them onto the back. Divide the rest of the marzipan into eight pieces and roll into legs 2 in long. Stick into place and leave to dry on waxed paper. Make brown eyes and a red mouth and stick in place.

3 Next make the spider's web. The glacé icing sets quickly, so have everything at hand. Sift the confectioners' sugar into a bowl, then gradually beat in the water. Place the bowl in a pan with hot, but not boiling, water. Heat gently and stir the icing; it should coat the back of the spoon. N.B. If the icing is too thick add a drop of water and if it is too thin add a little more sifted sugar. (Be careful not to overheat the icing.) Remove from the pan, dry the bowl and quickly pour two-thirds of the icing over the top of the cake. Spread to the edges with a palette knife. Tap the cake firmly on the work surface to flatten the icing.

4 Add a drop of brown coloring to the remaining icing and pour into a piping bag. Snip a tiny hole off the end and pipe concentric circles onto the cake, starting from the center and working outwards.

With a wooden toothpick, draw across the cake from the center outwards, dividing it into quarters. Then draw them from the edge of the cake inwards, dividing it into eighths. Leave to set.

5 Put the rest of the chocolate butter cream into a piping bag fitted with a star tube and pipe a border around the edge of the web. Put candles evenly around the border and the spider in the center.

Teddy's Birthday

After all the pieces have been assembled and stuck into the cake with a little water, an icing smoother is very useful to flatten the design.

INGREDIENTS
8 in round cake
¾ cup butter cream
apricot glaze
2¼ cups marzipan
3 cups white fondant
food colorings: brown, red, blue and
   black
¾ cup royal icing
silver balls

EQUIPMENT
10 in round cake board
No. 7 star tube
No. 7 shell tube
1¾ yards × 1 in wide ribbon
candles

apricot glaze

royal icing

fondant

ribbon

1 Split and fill the cake with butter cream. Place on the cake board and brush with hot apricot glaze. Cover with a layer of marzipan then fondant. Using a template, mark the design on top of the cake.

2 Color one-third of the remaining fondant pale brown. Color a piece pink, a piece red, some blue and a tiny piece black. Using a template, cut out the pieces and place in position on the cake. Stick down by lifting the edges carefully and brushing the undersides with a little water. Roll small ovals for the eyes and stick in place with the nose and eyebrows. Cut out a mouth and press flat.

3 Tie the ribbon round the cake. Color the royal icing blue and pipe the border around the base of the cake with the shell tube and tiny stars around the small cake with the star tube, inserting silver balls. Put the candles on the cake.

Party Teddy

There is very little piping on this cake. The teddy is built up with royal icing and colored coconut.

INGREDIENTS
8 in square cake
¾ cup butter cream
apricot glaze
3 cups marzipan
2¼ cups white fondant
½ cup shredded coconut
food colorings: blue and black
¾ cup royal icing

EQUIPMENT
10 in square cake board
1¾ yards × 1 in ribbon
candles

apricot glaze

fondant

shredded coconut

royal icing

1 Split and fill the cake with butter cream. Place on the cake board and brush with hot apricot glaze. Cover with a thin layer of marzipan then white fondant. Leave to dry overnight. Using a template, carefully mark position of the teddy onto the cake.

2 Put the coconut into a bowl and mix in a drop of blue coloring to color it pale blue. Spread a thin layer of royal icing within the lines and before it dries, sprinkle some pale blue coconut over the icing and press down lightly.

3 Roll out the fondant trimmings and cut out nose, ears and paws. Stick in place with a little royal icing. Stick the bow in place. Color a little royal icing black and pipe on eyes, nose and mouth. Pipe a white royal icing border around the base of the cake.

Hickory Dickory Dock

This appealing cake is based on the nursery rhyme. Small children love the jolly clockface, and the sugar mouse can be given as a prize.

INGREDIENTS
8 in round cake
6 in square cake
1 ½ cups butter cream
apricot glaze
4 ½ cups marzipan
3 cups brown fondant
¾ cup white fondant
food colorings: brown, gold, red, blue
    and black
2 silver balls
¼ cup royal icing

EQUIPMENT
10 × 14 in cake board
4 in piece of string
no. 1 writing tube

apricot glaze

silver balls

fondant

1 Split and fill the cakes with butter cream. Cut two wedges off one end of the square cake 2½ in from the corner.

2 Use a cake pan as a guide to cut a semi-circle from the opposite end of the square cake to fit around the round cake. Place on the cake board and brush with hot apricot glaze. Cover with a layer of marzipan then brown fondant.

3 Roll out half the white fondant and cut a 6 in circle for the face and a window for the pendulum. Cut out a 2 in long pendulum and 2 in and 2½ in long hands.

4 Paint the pendulum and hands gold and leave to dry overnight.

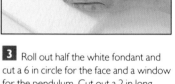

5 Color most of the remaining fondant pink and make a mouse with a string tail and silver balls for eyes. Leave to dry overnight on waxed paper.

6 Stick on the clock face with a little water. Using a template, mark the numbers and face onto the clock. Color the royal icing black and pipe the numbers with a no. 1 tube. Stick on the window with a little water. Roll out the excess brown fondant into long sausages and edge the face and the window. Color the remaining fondant blue, red and black. Roll out and cut the eyes, pupils, eyebrows, mouth and center. Stick on the hands, features and pendulum with a little water. Stick on the mouse.

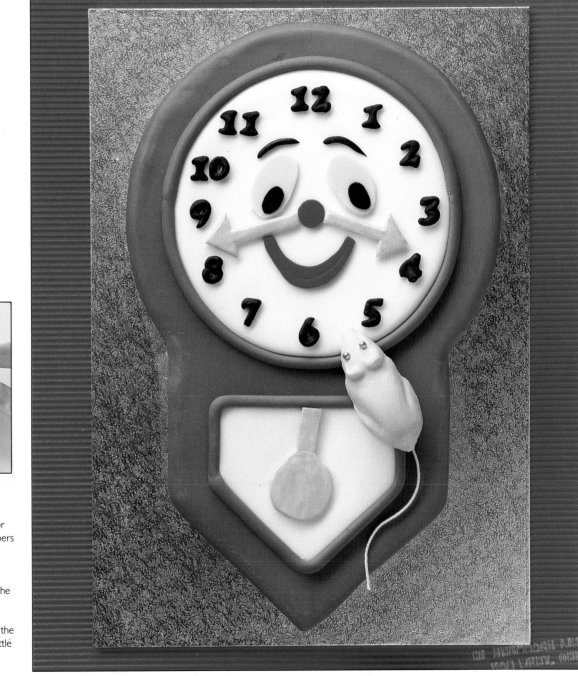

Noah's Ark

This charming cake is decorated with small purchased animals, about 1½ in high, available from party and cake decorating shops. Children will love to take home one of the novelties, as a reminder of the party.

INGREDIENTS
8 in square cake
¾ cup butter cream
apricot glaze
3 cups marzipan
3 cups light brown fondant
¾ cup royal icing
food colorings: brown, yellow and
    blue
chocolate mint stick

EQUIPMENT
10 in square cake board
rice paper flag
small animal cake ornaments

royal icing

apricot glaze

animal ornaments

fondant

chocolate mint stick

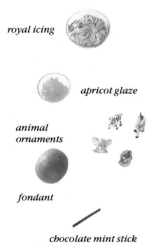

1 Split and fill the cake with butter cream. Cut a rectangle 8 × 5 in and cut to shape the hull of the boat. Place diagonally on the cake board.

4 Color one-third of the royal icing yellow and spread over the roof with a palette knife. Roughen it with a skewer to look like thatch.

2 Cut a smaller rectangle 4 × 2½ in for the cabin and a triangular roof from the remaining piece of cake. Sandwich together with butter cream or apricot glaze.

3 Cover the three pieces with a layer of marzipan then cover the hull and cabin with brown fondant. Sandwich together with butter cream and place in position on the hull. Roll a long sausage from the remaining brown fondant and stick round the edge of the hull with a little water. Mark planks of wood with the back of a knife. Leave to dry overnight.

5 Color the remaining royal icing blue and spread over the cake board, making rough waves. Stick a rice paper flag onto the chocolate mint stick and press on the back of the boat. Stick the small animals onto the boat with a dab of icing.

Magic Rabbit

This cheery rabbit bursting from a top hat is the perfect centerpiece for a magic theme party.

INGREDIENTS
2 × 6 in round cakes
1½ cups butter cream
¾ cup royal icing
apricot glaze
3 cups marzipan
4½ cups grey fondant
1½ cups pink marzipan
food colorings: black and pink
silver balls

EQUIPMENT
10 in square cake board
1¾ yards pink ribbon

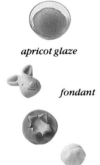

apricot glaze

fondant

marzipan

1 Split and fill the cakes with butter cream, then sandwich them one on top of the other. Stick on the center of the cake board with a little royal icing. Brush with hot apricot glaze. Cover with a thin layer of marzipan then with grey fondant, extending it 2 in over the board to form a hat brim. Lift and shape the sides, over the handles of wooden spoons, holding in place to dry.

2 With the remaining grey fondant, roll out to a 6 in circle, cut a cross in the center, place on the hat and curl triangles over a wooden spoon to shape. Smooth the join around the edge of the hat.

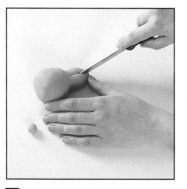

3 Shape the rabbit's head with pink marzipan, about 2 in in diameter, shaping a slightly pointed face. Mark the position of the eyes, nose and mouth. Shape the ears around the handle of a wooden spoon and leave to dry separately overnight.

4 Stick the rabbit in the center of the hat with a little royal icing. Tie the ribbon round the hat. Pipe a border of royal icing around the top and base of the hat and decorate with silver balls while the icing is still wet.

5 Color the remaining royal icing black and pipe the eyes and mouth.

Treasure Chest

Allow yourself a few days before the party to make this cake. The lock and handles are made separately, then left to dry for 48 hours before sticking onto the cake.

INGREDIENTS
8 in square cake
¾ cup butter cream
apricot glaze
2¼ cups marzipan
2¼ cups brown fondant
1 cup shredded coconut
¾ cup royal icing
food colorings: brown, green and
   black
edible gold dusting powder
3 tbsp white fondant
silver balls
chocolate money

EQUIPMENT
12 in round cake board

apricot glaze

silver balls

fondant

shredded coconut

chocolate money

1 Split and fill the cake with butter cream. Cut the cake in half and sandwich the halves on top of each other. Place on the cake board.

2 Cut the top to shape the rounded lid and brush with hot apricot glaze. Cover with a layer of marzipan then a layer of brown fondant.

3 Mark the lid of the treasure chest with a sharp knife.

4 Lay strips of fondant over the chest to mark the panels.

5 Put the coconut in a bowl and mix in a few drops of green coloring. Spread a little royal icing over the cake board and press the 'grass' lightly into it.

6 Cut out the padlock and handles. Cut a keyhole shape from the padlock and shape the handles over a small box. Leave to dry. Stick the padlock and handles into place with royal icing. Paint them gold and black and stick silver balls on the handles and padlock with a little royal icing to look like nails. Arrange the chocolate money around the chest on the grass.

Fairy Castle

Allow plenty of time to cover the cake with royal icing as it is quite a delicate job. If the icing dries too quickly, dip the palette knife into hot water to help smooth the surface.

INGREDIENTS
8 in round cake
¾ cup butter cream
apricot glaze
4½ cups marzipan
8 mini chocolate jelly rolls rolls
4½ cups royal icing
food colorings: pink, blue and green
Chuckles candies
4 ice cream cones
2 ice cream wafers
1 cup shredded coconut
marshmallows

EQUIPMENT
12 in square cake board
wooden toothpick

royal icing

ice cream cones

shredded coconut

Chuckles candies

apricot glaze

mini chocolate jelly rolls

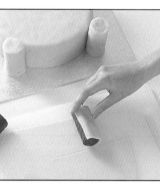

1 Split and fill the cake with butter cream, place in the center of the board and brush with hot apricot glaze. Cover with a layer of marzipan. Cover the jelly rolls separately with marzipan. Stick at regular intervals around the cake. Cut the remaining pieces of jelly roll in half.

2 Color two-thirds of the royal icing pale pink and spread evenly over the cake. Cover the extra pieces of jelly roll in icing and stick round the top of the cake. Using a toothpick, score the walls with brick patterns and stick Chuckles candies on the corner towers as windows. Cut the ice cream cones to fit the turrets and stick them in place. Leave to dry overnight.

3 Color half the remaining royal icing pale blue and spread thinly over the cones, using a fork to pattern the icing.

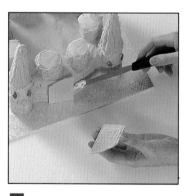

4 Cut the wafers to shape the gates, stick to the cake and cover with blue icing, marking planks with the back of a knife.

5 Put the coconut in a bowl and mix in a few drops of green coloring. Spread the board with the remaining royal icing and sprinkle over the coconut. Stick the marshmallows on the small turrets with a little royal icing.

Treasure Map

Allow several days to paint the map because each color must dry completely before adding another. Use a fairly dry paint brush to apply the color.

INGREDIENTS
10 in square cake
1½ cups butter cream
apricot glaze
3 cups marzipan
3 cups white fondant
1½ cups yellow fondant
food colorings: yellow, brown,
    paprika, green, black and red
¾ cup royal icing

EQUIPMENT
10 × 14 in cake board
no. 7 shell tube
no. 1 writing tube
soft paint brush

royal icing

apricot glaze

fondant

COOK'S TIP
Edible pens can also be used to mark the details on map. You may find them easier to handle than a paint brush.

1 Split and fill the cake with butter cream. Cut into an 8 × 10 in rectangle and place on the cake board. Brush with hot apricot glaze. Cover with a layer of marzipan then white fondant. Roll out the yellow fondant and cut in an uneven outline. Stick onto the cake with water and dry overnight. Mark out island, river, lake, mountains, trees etc. onto the map.

2 With brown and paprika colors and a fine paint brush, paint the edges of the map to look old and smudge the colors together with paper towelling. Paint the island pale green and the water around the island, river and lake pale blue. Dry overnight before painting on other details, otherwise the colors will run.

3 Pipe border of royal icing around the base of the cake with a shell tube. Color a little royal icing red and pipe the path to the treasure, marked with an 'X'. Color some icing green and pipe on grass and trees. Color some icing black and pipe on a North sign with a no. 1 tube.

Pirate's Hat

Black fondant may be purchased from specialist cake decorating shops. It is advisable to buy it ready-made rather than attempt to color it black yourself.

INGREDIENTS
10 in round cake
1½ cups butter cream
apricot glaze
3 cups marzipan
3 cups black fondant
¾ cup white fondant
food colorings: black and gold
chocolate money
hard candies

EQUIPMENT
12 in square cake board

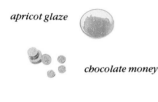

apricot glaze

chocolate money

fondant

hard candies

1 Split and fill the cake with butter cream. Cut in half and sandwich the halves together. Stand upright diagonally across the cake board and use a template to cut shallow dips to create the crown of the hat. Brush with hot apricot glaze.

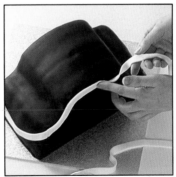

2 Cut a strip of marzipan to lay over the top of the cake to neaten the joints. Cover the whole cake with a layer of marzipan then black fondant.

3 Roll out the white fondant, cut ½ in strips and stick in place around the brim of the hat with a little water.

4 Mark the strip with a fork to look like braid. With a template, mark the skull and cross bones onto the hat. Cut the shapes out of the white fondant and stick in place with a little water. Paint the braid strip around the hat gold and arrange the chocolate money and hard candies around the board.

Royal Crown

The most difficult part of this cake is supporting the covered ice cream wafers with toothpicks while they dry in place. Plenty of royal icing can be used to smooth the joins and help to support the pieces.

INGREDIENTS
8 in round cake
6 in round cake
scant cup butter cream
apricot glaze
3 cups marzipan
3 cups white fondant
¾ cup red fondant
food coloring: red
3 cups royal icing
small black gum drops
4 ice cream fan wafers
silver balls
hard candies

EQUIPMENT
12 in square cake board
wooden toothpicks

fondant

ice cream fan wafers

silver balls

gum drops

hard candies

1 Split and fill the cakes with a little butter cream. Sandwich one on top of the other and place on the board. Shape the top cake into a dome. Brush with hot apricot glaze and cover with a layer of marzipan then white fondant.

2 Roll out the red fondant and cover the dome of the cake. Trim away the excess with a knife.

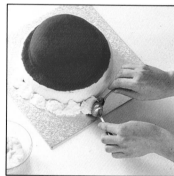

3 Spoon rough mounds of royal icing around the base of the cake and stick a black gum drop on each mound.

4 Cut the ice cream wafers in half.

5 Spread both sides of the wafers with royal icing and stick to the cake, smoothing the icing level with the sides of the cake. Use toothpicks to support until dry. Put silver balls on top of each point and hard candies around the sides of the crown, sticking in place with a little royal icing.

Fairy

This is one of the more advanced cakes and requires a lot of skill and patience. Allow yourself plenty of time if you are attempting the techniques for the first time.

INGREDIENTS
8 in round cake
¾ cup butter cream
apricot glaze
3 cups marzipan
2¾ cups pale blue fondant
¼ cup white fondant
food colorings: blue, pink, yellow and gold
½ cup royal icing
silver balls

EQUIPMENT
10 in cake board
no. 1 piping tube
fine paint brush, no. 2 or 3
twinkle pink sparkle luster powder
garrett frill cutter
small circle cutter
wooden toothpick
cottonwool
no. 7 star tube
silver ribbon

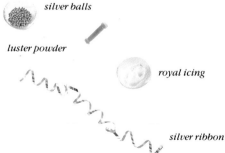

fondant

silver balls

luster powder

royal icing

silver ribbon

1 Split and fill the cake with butter cream. Place on the board and brush with hot apricot glaze. Cover with a thin layer of marzipan then pale blue fondant. Leave to dry overnight. Using a template, carefully mark the position of the fairy onto the cake. As royal icing dries quickly, work only on about 1 in sections of the fairy's wings at a time. Fill a piping bag with a no. 1 tube with white royal icing and carefully pipe over the outline of each wing section.

2 Pipe a second line just inside that and with a damp paint brush, brush long strokes from the edges towards the center, leaving more icing at the edges and fading away to a thin film near the base of the wings. Leave to dry for 1 hour. Brush with dry luster powder (not dissolved in spirit).

3 Color a little fondant pink, roll and cut out the body. Lay carefully in position. Dampen a paint brush, remove the excess water on paper towelling and carefully brush under the arms, legs and head to stick. Round off any sharp edges by rubbing gently with a finger. Cut out the bodice and shoes and stick in place. Cut out a wand and star and leave to dry.

4 Work quickly to make the tutu, as thin fondant dries quickly and will crack easily. Each frill must be made separately. Roll out a small piece of fondant to ⅛ in thick and cut out a fluted circle with a small plain inner circle. (The depth of the frill will be governed by the size of the central hole; the smaller the central hole, the wider the frill.)

5 Cut into quarters and with a wooden toothpick, roll along the fluted edge to stretch it and give fullness.

6 Attach the frills to the waist with a little water. Repeat with the other layers, tucking the sides under neatly. Use a wooden toothpick to arrange the frills and small pieces of cotton wool to hold the folds of the skirt in place until dry. Leave to dry overnight. Brush a little luster powder over the edge of the tutu. Paint on the hair and face, stick on the wand and star and paint the star gold. Pipe a border of royal icing round the edge of the board with a star nozzle and place a silver ball on each point. Leave to dry. Color a little royal icing yellow and pipe over the hair. Paint with a touch of gold coloring.

Pinball Machine

Allow plenty of time to decorate this cake and remember to keep all the different colored fondants tightly wrapped in separate pieces of plastic wrap to prevent them drying out.

INGREDIENTS
10 in square cake
1½ cups butter cream
apricot glaze
3 cups marzipan
¾ cup royal icing
3 cups white fondant
food colorings: yellow, blue, green and pink
candies
2 ice cream fan wafers

EQUIPMENT
12 in square cake board
no. 1 writing tube

apricot glaze

candies

ice cream fan wafers

butter cream

1 Split and fill the cake with butter cream. Cut off 2 in strip from one side and reserve.

2 Using a sharp serrated knife, cut a thin wedge off the top of the cake, diagonally along its length, to end just above the half way mark. This will give a sloping top.

3 Using an 8 in cake pan as a guide, cut an arched back from the reserved cake. Brush cakes with hot apricot glaze. Cover separately with a layer of marzipan and place on the board, sticking together with royal icing. Leave to dry overnight.

4 Cover with a layer of fondant. Leave to dry. Using a template, mark out a design on top of the cake. Color the fondant in different colors, roll out and cut to fit each section. Stick with water and smooth the joins carefully.

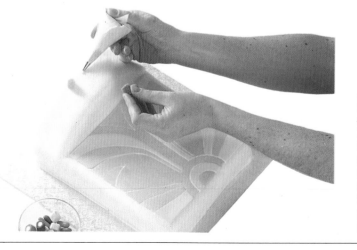

5 Use royal icing to stick different candies on the cake as buffers, flippers, lights and knobs. Roll some blue fondant into a long sausage and edge the pinball table and divider. Cut a zig-zag design for the sides and a small screen for the back. Stick on with water. Stick the ice cream fans at the back of the screen. Load the pinball candies and stick run-out letters or pipe the name on the screen.

Camping Tent

The perfect cake for the eager camper. You may find it easier to cover the sides of the cake first, and then the top, rather than all in one.

INGREDIENTS
8 in square cake
¾ cup butter cream
apricot glaze
3 cups marzipan
¼ cup brown fondant
3 cups orange fondant
food colorings: orange, brown, green, red, yellow and blue
¾ cup royal icing
1 cup shredded coconut
chocolate matchsticks

EQUIPMENT
10 in square cake board
wooden toothpicks
fine paint brush
no. 1 plain tube
basket weave tube

apricot glaze

shredded coconut

fondant

1 Split and fill the cake with a little butter cream. Cut the cake in half. Cut one half in two diagonally from the top right edge to the bottom left edge to form the roof of the tent.

2 Stick the two wedges, back to back, on top of the oblong with hot apricot glaze to form the tent. Measure the height from the 'ground' and trim off at 4 in high. Use these trimmings on either side of the base. Place the cake diagonally on the board and brush with hot apricot glaze.

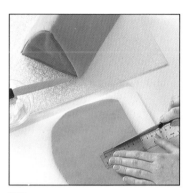

3 Cover with a layer of marzipan. Cover one end of the tent with brown fondant and cover the rest with orange fondant. It is easier to cut the opening for the tent separately and then stick on with a little water. Cut a 3 in slit down the front of the tent, lay over the brown fondant then trim off the excess and smooth the joins at the top. Fold back the sides and secure with royal icing. Leave to dry. Stick halved toothpicks in the corners of the tent as pegs and in the ridge as tent poles.

4 Put the coconut in a bowl and mix in a little green coloring. Spread the cake board with a thin layer of royal icing and sprinkle with the coconut.

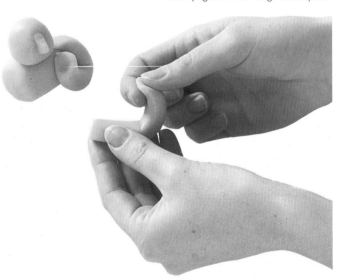

5 Color ⅓ cup of marzipan pink, roll a ball for the head, a tiny wedge for the nose and shape the body and arms. Paint a blue T-shirt on to the body and leave to dry. Color some of the royal icing brown and pipe on the hair with a basket weave tube. Pipe on the mouth and eyes. Make a bonfire with broken chocolate matchsticks.

Sailing Boat

For chocolate lovers, make a chocolate-flavored sponge by substituting 2 oz cocoa powder for the same quantity of flour.

INGREDIENTS
8 in square cake
1½ cups butter cream
1 tbsp cocoa powder
4 large chocolate fingers
¾ cup royal icing
food coloring: blue

EQUIPMENT
10 in square cake board
rice paper
round circle cutter
red and blue powder tints
paint brush
plastic drinking straw
wooden toothpick
2 small cake ornaments

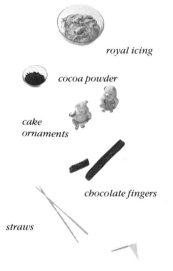

royal icing

cocoa powder

cake
ornaments

chocolate fingers

straws

toothpicks

1 Split and fill the cake with half the butter cream. Cut an 8 × 5 in rectangle from the cake. Cut the rectangle to shape the hull of the boat and place diagonally across the cake board. Sift the cocoa and mix well into the remaining butter cream. Spread the chocolate buttercream evenly over the top and sides of the boat.

2 Split the chocolate fingers lengthways and press horizontally into the icing to resemble planks of wood. Cut a flake in short lengths for the rudder and tiller and place at the stern of the boat. Sprinkle the crumbs over the top.

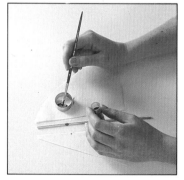

3 To make the sails, cut a piece of rice paper 5½ × 6½ in and another piece 6 × 3 in. With sharp scissors, cut the large sail in a gentle curve, starting at the top and working down to the widest part of the paper. Cut the smaller one into a

triangle. Using the round cutter to contain the powder tint, gently brush onto the smooth side of the rice paper, working it in carefully. Remove the cutter. Cut a triangular flag and color red. (Do not use liquid colors.) Wet the edges of the rice paper and stick onto the straw, holding in position until stuck. Make a hole for the straw 3 in from the bow of the boat and push into the cake about 1 in with the small sail at the front and the large one at the back. Stick the flag onto a wooden toothpick and insert it into the straw. Color the royal icing blue and spread on the board in waves. Place the small ornaments on the boat.

Sand Castle

Crushed wheatmeal biscuits are used to cover this fun cake. It is ideal for children who do not like the richness of butter cream as only a very small amount is used to sandwich the cake.

INGREDIENTS
6 in round cake
¾ cup butter cream
apricot glaze
⅔ cup wheatmeal biscuits
¾ cup royal icing
food coloring: blue
candies

EQUIPMENT
10 in square cake board
rice paper
plastic drinking straw
candles

royal icing

apricot glaze

candies

wheatmeal biscuits

butter cream

1 Split the cakes, then sandwich all the layers with butter cream, one on top of the other. Place in the center of the cake board. Cut 1 ¼ in off the top just above the filling and shape the rest of the cake with slightly sloping sides.

2 Cut 1 ¼ in cubes from the reserved piece and stick on for the turrets. Brush with hot apricot glaze.

3 Crush the wheatmeal biscuits and press through a sieve to make the 'sand'. Press on the crushed biscuits, using a palette knife to get a smooth finish. Color some royal icing blue and spread around the sand castle on the board to make a moat. Spread a little royal icing around the board and sprinkle on sand. Make a flag with rice paper and half a straw and stick into the cake. Stick candles into each turret and arrange the candies on the board.

Computer Game

This is a small cake to give to a computer game fanatic. The fine rope is made by rolling the fondant on a smooth surface with an icing smoother to give a neat continuous finish.

INGREDIENTS
6 in square cake
¾ cup butter cream
apricot glaze
1½ cups marzipan
1½ cups black fondant
¼ cup white fondant
food colorings: black, blue, red and yellow
royal icing

EQUIPMENT
8 in square cake board
wooden toothpick
fine paint brush

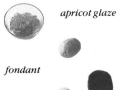

apricot glaze

fondant

butter cream

1 Split and fill the cake with a little butter cream. With a sharp serrated knife, cut 1 in off one side of the cake and ½ in off the other. Round the corners slightly. Place on the cake board and brush with hot apricot glaze.

2 Cover with a layer of marzipan then black fondant. With a wooden toothpick mark the speaker holes and position of screen and knobs. Color half the white fondant pale blue, roll out and cut out a 2½ in square for the screen. Stick in the center of the game with a little water. Color a small piece red and the rest yellow. Cut out the start switch 1 in long from the red and the controls from the yellow. Stick into position with water. Roll the remaining black fondant into a long, thin sausage and edge the screen and around the base of the cake.

3 With a fine paint brush, draw the game onto the screen with a little blue color. Pipe letters onto the buttons with a little royal icing.

Sheet of Music

This cake is ideal for young musicians. As it requires very delicate piping, it is advisable to practice first before attempting this cake.

INGREDIENTS
10 in square cake
1½ cups butter cream
apricot glaze
3 cups marzipan
3 cups white fondant
¾ cup royal icing
food coloring: black

EQUIPMENT
10 × 12 in cake board
no. 0 writing tube
no. 7 shell tube
1½ yards ribbon

apricot glaze

royal icing

fondant

1 Split and fill the cake with a little butter cream. Cut 2 in off one side of the cake so that it measures 8 × 10 in. Place on the cake board and brush with hot apricot glaze. Cover with a layer of marzipan then white fondant. Leave to dry overnight.

2 With a template, mark out the sheet of music and child's name.

3 Pipe the lines and bars first with white royal icing and a no. 0 tube then color the remaining icing black and pipe the clefs, name and notes. Pipe a royal icing border around the base of the cake with the shell tube and tie a ribbon around the sides.

Doll's House

Little children love this cake. Pipe their age on the door. The same number of candles can be added to the cake if you wish.

INGREDIENTS
10 in square cake
1½ cups butter cream
apricot glaze
3 cups marzipan
3 cups white fondant
food colorings: red, yellow, blue, black, green and gold
¾ cup royal icing

EQUIPMENT
12 in square cake board
no. 2 writing tube
flower decorations

apricot glaze

flowers

fondant

1 Split and fill the cake with butter cream. Cut 2½ in triangles off two corners then use these pieces to make a chimney. Place on the cake board and brush with hot apricot glaze. Cover with a layer of marzipan then white fondant.

2 Using a pastry wheel, mark the roof to look like thatch. Mark the chimney with the back of a knife to look like bricks.

3 Paint the chimney red and the roof yellow.

4 Mark the door 3 × 4½ in and the windows 2½ in square. Color 2 tbsp of fondant red, cut out and stick on the door with a little water. Color a small piece blue, cut out and stick on for the top fanlight. Paint on the curtains with blue food coloring. Color half the royal icing black and pipe the window frames and panes, around the door and the fanlight.

5 Color the remaining royal icing green. Pipe the flowers under the windows and the climber up the wall and onto the roof. Stick the flowers in place with a little icing and pipe green flower centers. Pipe the age of the child on the door. Leave to dry for 1 hour. Paint the knocker, handle and number with gold food coloring.

Circus

This design is very easy to achieve. The miniature circus ornaments measure 2 in high and can be bought from party shops, although anything similar can be used.

INGREDIENTS
8 in round cake
¾ cup butter cream
apricot glaze
3 cups marzipan
3 cups white fondant
food colorings: red and blue
¾ cup royal icing
3 wheatmeal biscuits
silver balls

EQUIPMENT
10 in round cake board
no. 5 star tube
small plastic circus ornaments

apricot glaze

wheatmeal biscuits

fondant

silver balls

1 Split and fill the cake with a little butter cream. Place on the cake board and brush with hot apricot glaze. Cover with a layer of marzipan then white fondant. Color ¾ cup of fondant pink, roll into a rope and stick around the top edge of the cake to make a wall.

2 Color half the remaining fondant red and the other half blue. Roll out each color and cut into twelve 1 in squares. Stick alternately at an angle around the side of the cake with a little water. Pipe stars around the base of the cake with royal icing and stick in silver balls as you work.

3 Crush the wheatmeal biscuits by pressing through a sieve to make the 'sand'. Scatter over the top of the cake and place small circus ornaments on top.

Drum

This is a colorful cake for very young children. The ropes can be made by rolling by hand on a smooth work surface, but an icing smoother gives a much better result.

INGREDIENTS
6 in round cake
¼ cup butter cream
apricot glaze
2¼ cups marzipan
3 cups white fondant
food colorings: red, blue and yellow

EQUIPMENT
8 in round cake board

marzipan

apricot glaze

butter cream

fondant

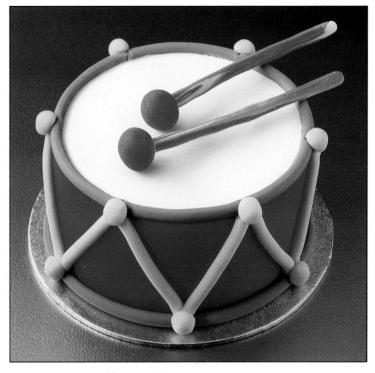

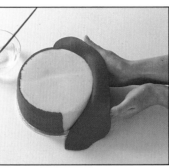

1 Split and fill the cake with a little butter cream. Place on the cake board and brush with hot apricot glaze. Cover with a layer of marzipan and leave to dry overnight. Color half the fondant red. Roll out to 10 × 12 in and cut in half. Stick to the sides of the cake with water, smoothing the joins neatly.

2 Roll out a circle of white fondant to fit the top of the cake and divide the rest in half. Color one half blue and the other yellow. Divide the blue into four equal pieces and roll each piece into a sausage long enough to go half way around the cake. Stick around the base and top of the cake with a little water.

3 Mark the cake into six around the top and bottom using waxed paper marked in six wedges.

4 Roll the yellow fondant into strands long enough to cross diagonally from top to bottom to form the drum strings. Roll the rest of the yellow fondant into 12 small balls and stick where the strings join the drum. Using red and white fondant, knead together until streaky and roll two balls and sticks 6 in long. Dry overnight. Stick together with royal icing to make the drumsticks and place on top of the drum.

Clown Face

Children love this happy clown. His frilly collar is quite easy to make, but you do have to work quickly before the fondant dries.

INGREDIENTS
8 in round cake
¾ cup butter cream
apricot glaze
3 cups marzipan
3 cups white fondant
¾ cup royal icing
food colorings: pink, red, green, blue
    and black
silver balls

EQUIPMENT
10 in round cake board
no. 8 star tube
garrett frill cutter
small circle cutter
wooden toothpick
cottonwool
candles

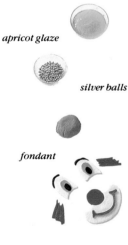

apricot glaze

silver balls

fondant

candles

1 Split and fill the cake with butter cream. Place in the center of the cake board and brush with hot apricot glaze. Cover with a thin layer of marzipan then white fondant. Mark the position of the features. Pipe stars around base of the cake with royal icing, placing silver balls as you work, and leave to dry overnight.

2 Color half the remaining fondant pale pink, roll out and with the use of a template, cut out the shape of the face. Lay on the cake with the top of the head touching one edge of the cake.

3 Color the remaining pink fondant red, roll out and cut out the nose. Roll out some of the white fondant, cut out the eyes and mouth and stick on the face with the nose, using a little water. Roll out a little of the red fondant into a thin sausage and cut to fit the mouth. Stick in place with a little water.

4 Roll out the rest of the red fondant, cut in thin strands for hair and stick in place with water.

5 Color most of the remaining fondant pale green and roll out thinly. Cut out a fluted circle with a small plain inner circle. Cut through one side and roll along the fluted edge with a toothpick to stretch it. Stick on the cake with a little water and arrange the frills. Repeat to make three layers of frills, holding them in place with cotton wool until dry.

6 Color a little fondant blue, roll and cut out eyes and stick in place with a little water. Color the rest of the fondant black, roll and cut out the eyes and eye-brows, then stick in position. Place the candles at the top of the head.

Kite

The happy face on this cheerful kite uses the same template pattern as the Clown Face cake, and is a great favorite with children of all ages.

INGREDIENTS
10 in square cake
1½ cups butter cream
apricot glaze
3 cups marzipan
3 cups pale yellow fondant
1½ cups white fondant
¾ cup royal icing
food colorings: yellow, red, green, blue and black

EQUIPMENT
12 in square cake board
no. 8 star tube
candles

apricot glaze

royal icing

fondant

1 Split and fill the cake with butter cream. Mark 6 in from one corner down two sides and using a ruler from this point cut down to the opposite corner on both sides to get the kite shape. Place diagonally on the cake board and brush with hot apricot glaze.

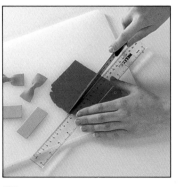

4 To make the kite's tail, roll out each color separately and cut two 1½ × ½ in lengths from the blue, red and green fondants. Pinch them to shape into bows.

2 Cover with a layer of marzipan then pale yellow fondant. Using a template, mark the face on the kite. Divide the white fondant into four and color them red, green, blue and black. Wrap each separately in plastic wrap. Pipe a border of shells around the base of the cake.

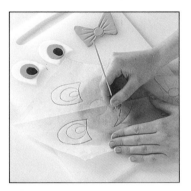

3 Using a template, cut out the face, bow tie and buttons and stick in place with a little water.

5 Roll the yellow into a long rope and lay it on the board in a wavy line from the narrow end of the kite and stick the bows in place with water. Roll balls of yellow fondant, stick on the board with a little royal icing and press in the candles.

Balloons

This is a simple yet effective design that can be adapted to any age. Young children like it especially.

INGREDIENTS
8 in round cake
¾ cup butter cream
apricot glaze
3 cups marzipan
3 cups white fondant
food colorings: pink, blue, green and
   yellow
¾ cup royal icing

EQUIPMENT
10 in cake board
1¾ yards × ½ in wide ribbon
no. 2 plain tube
no. 7 star tube
candles

apricot glaze

fondant

ribbon

1 Split and fill the cake with butter cream. Place on the cake board and brush with hot apricot glaze. Cover with a layer of marzipan then white fondant. Divide the remaining fondant into three pieces; color one pink, one blue and the other green. Roll out and, using a template, cut out a balloon from each color. Stick onto cake with a little water, rubbing the edges gently with a finger to round off straight edges.

2 Tie the ribbon round the cake. With yellow royal icing and a plain tube, pipe on the strings, attaching them to the balloons. Pipe a border around the base of the cake.

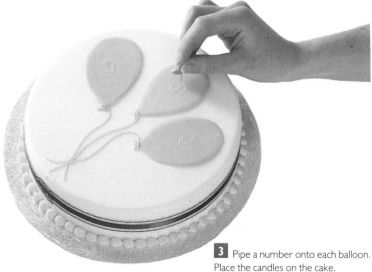

3 Pipe a number onto each balloon. Place the candles on the cake.

Wading Pool

This fun cake will need at least a day's preparation before the party; the boat and duck are modeled from fondant and the bather from marzipan. The decorations are left to dry overnight before arranging them in the royal icing before it has completely dried.

INGREDIENTS
6 in round cake
¼ cup butter cream
apricot glaze
2¼ cups marzipan
3 cups white fondant
food colorings: blue, red, yellow,
    green and brown
¾ cup royal icing

EQUIPMENT
8 in round cake board
no. 1 plain tube
basket weave tube

apricot glaze

royal icing

fondant

drinking straws

1 Split and fill the cake with a little butter cream. Place in the center of the cake board and brush with hot apricot glaze. Cover with a layer of marzipan then white fondant. Divide the remaining fondant into four pieces and color them blue, red, yellow and green. Shape a small duck from the yellow, a 1½ in rubber ring from the red and a boat from the green. Roll the remains of each color into two sausages long enough to go half way around the cake. Stick to the sides of the cake with a little water, flattening slightly and smoothing the joins so the stripes come to the top of the cake.

2 Color ⅓ cup of marzipan pink and shape into a small child with a head, half a body, arms and feet. Place into the rubber ring and leave to dry overnight.

3 Color two-thirds of the royal icing blue and spread on top of the cake to resemble water, placing the child, duck and boat in the water. Color a little royal icing brown and pipe on the child's hair using a basket weave pipe. Pipe the eyes and mouth.

Chess Board

For this cake to look most effective, the squares have to have very sharp edges, so take care to neaten them as you stick them into position.

INGREDIENTS
10 in square cake
1½ cups butter cream
apricot glaze
5¾ cups marzipan
3 cups white fondant
food colorings: black and red
silver balls
¾ cup black fondant
¾ cup royal icing

EQUIPMENT
12 in square cake board
no. 8 star tube

apricot glaze

silver balls

fondant

1 Split and fill the cake with butter cream. Place on the cake board and brush with hot apricot glaze. Roll out 3 cups of marzipan and cover the cake with a layer of marzipan then white fondant. Leave to dry overnight.

2 Divide the remaining marzipan in half and color one half black and the other half red. To shape the chess pieces, work with one color at a time. Roll ¼ cup of marzipan into a sausage and cut into 8 equal pieces then shape into pawns.

Divide ⅔ cup of marzipan into 6 equal pieces then shape into two castles, two knights and two bishops. Divide 2 tbsp of marzipan in half and shape a queen and a king. Decorate with silver balls. Dry overnight.

3 Mark the cake into eight 1¼ in squares along each side, leaving a border around the edge. Divide the board into 64 equal squares using a sharp knife.

4 Roll out the black fondant and cut into 1¼ in squares. Stick onto alternate squares on the board with a little water, starting with a black square in the bottom left hand corner and finishing with another black square in the top right hand corner.

5 Cut ½ in black strips to edge the board and stick in place with a little water. Pipe a border round the base of the cake with royal icing. Place the chess pieces in position.

Jack-in-the-Box

For a change, tiny edible flowers or letters can be stuck onto the sides of the box.

INGREDIENTS
6 in square cake
¼ cup butter cream
apricot glaze
2¼ cups marzipan
3 cups white fondant
ice cream cone
¾ cup royal icing
food colorings: blue, black, green, red
    and yellow
silver balls

EQUIPMENT
8 in round cake board
garrett frill cutter
plain circle cutter
wooden toothpick
cottonwool
no. 8 star tube

silver balls

royal icing

ice cream cone

fondant

1 Split and fill the cake with butter cream. Cut a 2 in rectangle from two sides of the cake to create a 4 in square, a 2 in square and two rectangles. Sandwich the rectangles together on top of the large square to make a cube. Place on the cake board and brush with hot apricot glaze. Cover with a layer of marzipan then white fondant. Shape the remaining cube of cake into a ball for the head. Brush with hot apricot glaze, cover with marzipan then white fondant. Leave to dry overnight.

2 Cut the top off the ice cream cone. Stick the wide part of the cone in the center of the cake with a little royal icing then stick the head on top.

3 Color a small piece of fondant blue, roll out and cut a fluted circle with a small inner circle. (The depth of the frill will depend on the size of the central hole; the smaller the center, the wider the frill.) Cut one side and open out then roll the fluted edge with a wooden toothpick to stretch it. Attach it to the neck with royal icing, carefully arranging the folds with a toothpick and supporting with cottonwool while they dry. Make a second frill in the same way.

4 Stick the ice cream cone hat on the head with a little royal icing. Cut eyes from blue fondant and stick on with a little water. Color pieces of fondant black, green and red and roll out. Cut and stick on black eyes. Cut a semi-circle of green, stick around the back of the head and snip with sharp scissors to give spikey hair (or cut two short lengths). Cut out red nose, mouth and numbers for the sides of the box. Stick on with a little water.

5 Color the remaining royal icing yellow and pipe stars round the edges of the cube and pompoms on the hat, sticking in silver balls as you go.

Toy Car

This little car can be made for any age. You could add a personalized number plate with the child's name and age to the back of the car.

INGREDIENTS
8 in round cake
¾ cup butter cream
apricot glaze
3 cups marzipan
3 cups yellow fondant
¼ cup red fondant
food colorings: yellow, red and black
2 tbsp royal icing
candies

EQUIPMENT
10 in round cake board
no. 1 writing tube
candies

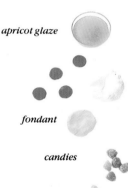

apricot glaze

fondant

candies

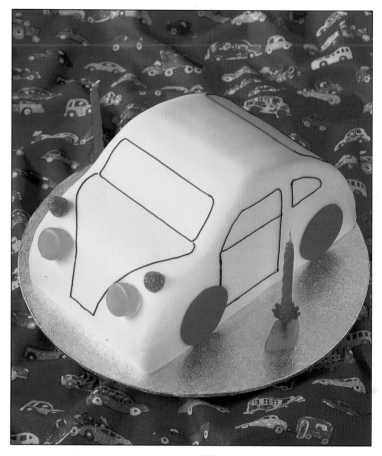

1 Split and fill the cake with a little butter cream. Cut in half and sandwich the halves upright together. With a sharp serrated knife, cut a shallow dip to create the wind-screen and to shape the bonnet. Place on the cake board and brush with hot apricot glaze. Cut a strip of marzipan to cover the top of the cake to level the joins. Then cover with a layer of marzipan then yellow fondant. Leave to dry overnight.

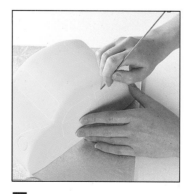

2 Mark the doors and windows onto the car with a sharp skewer.

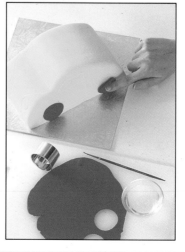

3 Roll out the red fondant and cut out four 1½ in wheels with a cutter. Stick in place with a little water. Mark the center of each wheel with a smaller cutter. Color the royal icing black and pipe over the doors and windows. Stick on candies for headlights with a little royal icing. Press the candles into candies and stick to the board with a little royal icing.

Racing Track

This cake will delight all eight-year-old racing car enthusiasts. It's relatively simple to make and can be decorated with as many cars as you like.

INGREDIENTS
2 × 6 in round cakes
¾ cup butter cream
apricot glaze
3 cups marzipan
3 cups pale blue fondant
¼ cup white fondant
food colorings: blue and red
¾ cup royal icing

EQUIPMENT
10 × 14 in cake board
2 in fluted cutter
no. 8 star tube
no. 2 plain tube
candles
2 small racing cars

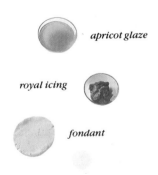

apricot glaze

royal icing

fondant

1 Split and fill the cakes with a little butter cream. Cut off a ½ in piece from one side of each cake and place the cakes on the cake board with the flat edges together. Brush with hot apricot glaze. Cover with a layer of marzipan then pale blue fondant.

2 Mark a 2 in circle in the center of each cake. Roll out the white fondant and cut out two fluted circles and stick in the marked spaces.

3 Color the royal icing red. Pipe a shell border around the base of the cake using a no. 8 star tube. Pipe a track for the cars on the cake using a no. 2 plain tube and place the candles on the two white circles. Place the cars on the track.

Fire Engine

This jolly fire engine is simplicity itself as the decorations are mainly bought candies and novelties. Because the fondant is bought ready-colored the cake is very quick to prepare.

INGREDIENTS
8 in square cake
¾ cup butter cream
apricot glaze
2¼ cups marzipan
2¼ cups red fondant
liquorice strips
¾ cup royal icing
food colorings: black and green
¾ cup white fondant
candies
2 silver bells
1 cup shredded coconut

EQUIPMENT
10 in round cake board
no. 2 plain tube
candles

liquorice strips

candies

fondant

liquorice wheel

1 Split and fill the cake with a little butter cream. Cut in half and sandwich one half on top of the other. Place on the cake board and brush with apricot glaze.

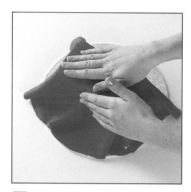

2 Cover the entire cake with a layer of marzipan and red fondant.

3 Mark the windows, ladder and wheels.

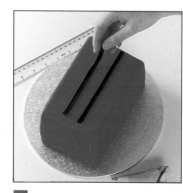

4 To make the ladder, cut the liquorice into two strips and short pieces for the rungs. Color half the royal icing black and stick the ladder to the top of the cake with royal icing. Roll out the white fondant, cut out and stick on the windows with a little water.

5 Pipe around the windows in black royal icing. Stick candies in place for headlights, lamps and wheels and stick the silver bells on the roof. Put the coconut in a bowl and mix in a few drops of green coloring. Spread a little royal icing over the cake board and sprinkle with coconut. Stick candies to the board with royal icing and press in the candles.

Army Tank

The camouflage fondant can be laid over the cake in sections and the joins smoothed neatly.

INGREDIENTS
10 in square cake
1½ cups butter cream
apricot glaze
3 cups marzipan
2¼ cups green fondant
¾ cup brown fondant
food colorings: green and brown
chocolate finger
4 tbsp royal icing
round cookies
candies
liquorice strips

EQUIPMENT
10 × 14 in cake board

apricot glaze

chocolate finger

fondant

cookies

1 Split and fill the cake with butter cream. Cut off a 6 in rectangle from one side of the cake. Cut a smaller rectangle 6 × 3 in and stick on the top.

2 Using a sharp serrated knife, shape the sloping top and cut a 1 in piece from both ends between the tracks. Shape the rounded ends for the wheels and track. Assemble the cake on the cake board and brush with hot apricot glaze. Cover with a layer of marzipan. Roll out the green fondant to about a 10 in square. Break small pieces of brown fondant and place all over the green. Flatten and roll out together to give the camouflage effect.

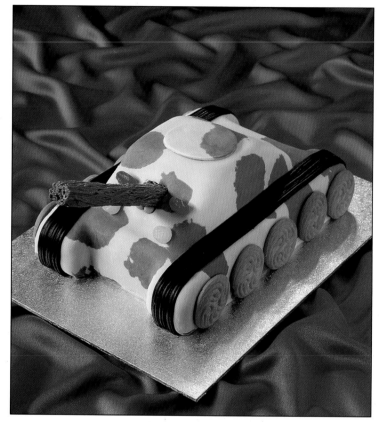

3 Turn the icing over, brush off excess sugar and repeat on the underside. Continue to roll out until the fondant is about ⅛ in thick. Lay the fondant over the cake, gently pressing over the turret and down the sides of the track on both sides. Then carefully mold over the tracks, cutting away the excess. Cut a piece into a 2½ in disk and stick on with a little water for the hatch on top. Cut a small hole for the gun and stick the chocolate finger in for the gun. Stick liquorice for the tracks, using a little black royal icing. Stick on cookies for the wheels and candies for the lights and port holes.

Number 6 Cake

Use the round pan as a guide to cut the square cake to fit neatly around the round cake.

INGREDIENTS
6 in round cake
6 in square cake
¾ cup butter cream
apricot glaze
3 cups marzipan
3 cups pale yellow fondant
¼ cup pale green fondant
food colorings: yellow and green
¾ cup royal icing

EQUIPMENT
10 × 14 in cake board
no. 1 plain tube
no. 8 star tube
3 in fluted cutter
plastic train set with 6 candles

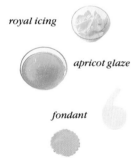

royal icing

apricot glaze

fondant

1 Split and fill the cakes with a little butter cream. Cut the square cake in half and cut a rounded end from one oblong to fit neatly around the round cake. Trim the cakes to the same depth and assemble on the cake board as shown, and brush with hot apricot glaze. Cover with a thin layer of marzipan. Smooth any joins and make sure surface is flat.

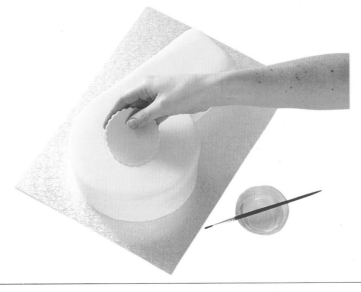

2 Roll out and cover the cake with pale yellow fondant. Mark a 3 in circle in the center of the round cake. Color a small piece of fondant pale green, roll out and cut out a fluted circle. Stick in place with water and dry overnight. Mark the track ¾ in wide or width of the train. Color royal icing yellow and pipe track with a no. 1 tube. Using a no. 8 star tube, pipe a border around base and top of the cake. Pipe the name on the green circle and attach the train with royal icing.

Space Ship

For this cake the triangles for the jets should be covered separately, then stuck into position after decorating.

INGREDIENTS
10 in square cake
1½ cups butter cream
apricot glaze
2¼ cups marzipan
3 cups white fondant
food colorings: blue, pink and black

EQUIPMENT
12 in square cake board
candles
gold paper stars

apricot glaze

fondant

candles

1 Split and fill the cake with a little butter cream. With a sharp serrated knife, cut a 4 in piece diagonally across the middle of the cake and about 10 in long.

2 Shape the nose and cut the remaining cake in three 3 in triangles for the sides and top of the ship. Cut two smaller triangles for the boosters and any remaining cake to fit down the middle of the space ship. Assemble diagonally across the cake board and brush with hot apricot glaze. Cover with a layer of marzipan then white fondant.

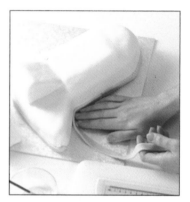

3 Color one-third of the remaining fondant blue, one-third pink and one-third black. Wrap each separately in plastic wrap. Roll out the blue and cut in ½ in strips. Stick in a continuous line around the base of the cake with a little water and outline the triangles. Cut a 1 in strip and stick down the center of the space ship.

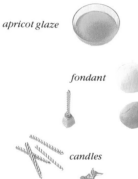

4 Roll out the pink fondant and cut out shapes to decorate the ship. Roll out the black fondant and cut out windows, circles, name and numbers. Stick in place with a little water.

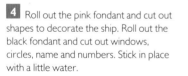

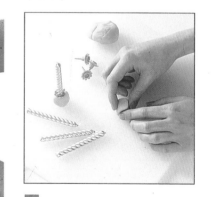

5 With any leftover fondant, make candle holders by shaping into small cubes. Stick the candles into them then stick onto the board. Decorate the board with gold stars.

Ballerina

This cake requires patience and plenty of time for the decoration. The tiny flowers were made with ¼ in and ⅜ in flower cutters with ejectors.

INGREDIENTS
8 in round cake
¾ cup butter cream
apricot glaze
3 cups marzipan
3 cups white fondant
food colorings: pink, yellow and green
¾ cup royal icing

EQUIPMENT
10 in round cake board
small flower cutter
garrett frill cutter
small circle cutter
wooden toothpick
cottonwool
fine paint brush
no. 7 shell tube
1¾ yards ribbon

apricot glaze

royal icing

fondant

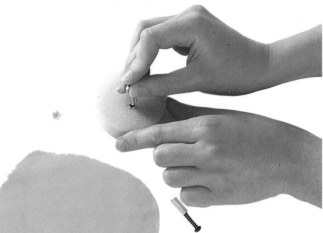

1 Split and fill the cake with butter cream. Place on the board and brush with hot apricot glaze. Cover with a layer of marzipan then a layer of white fondant. Leave to dry overnight. Divide the remaining fondant into three; color one flesh tones and the other two contrasting pinks for the tutu and flowers. Roll out each color separately and cut out 6 flowers and 3 tiny flowers from the paler pink fondant for the headdress. Leave aside to dry.

2 Using the template, carefully mark the position of the ballerina onto the cake. Cut out the body from flesh colored fondant and stick into position with a little water. Round off edges by rubbing gently with a finger. Cut out a bodice from the darker pink fondant and stick in place.

3 To make the tutu, work quickly as the thin fondant dries quickly and will crack. Roll out the darker pink fondant to ⅛ in thick and cut out a fluted circle with a small plain inner circle.

4 Cut the circle into quarters and with a wooden toothpick, roll along the fluted edge to stretch it and give fullness.

5 Attach the frills to the waist with a little water. Repeat with two more layers, using a toothpick to shape the frills and cottonwool to hold them in place until dry. For the final layer, use the paler pink and cover with a short dark frill, as the bodice extension. Leave to dry overnight.

6 Attach flowers to the hoop. Color a little royal icing green and pipe tiny leaves in between. Paint on the face and hair. Stick three tiny flowers in place around the head. Cut pale pink fondant shoes and stick in place with water, and paint ribbons. Color a little royal icing dark pink and pipe the flower centers on the hoop and headdress. Pipe white royal icing around the base of the cake with the shell tube and tie round the ribbon.

Toy Telephone

This is a small cake for children, with the numbers on the dial representing their age. The child's name can be piped in a contrasting color.

INGREDIENTS
6 in square cake
¼ cup butter cream
apricot glaze
2 cups marzipan
2¼ cups white fondant
food colorings: yellow, blue, red and
    black
liquorice strips
¾ cup royal icing

EQUIPMENT
8 in square cake board
no. 1 writing tube

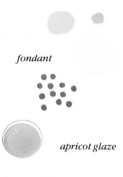

fondant

apricot glaze

liquorice strips

1 Split and fill the cake with butter cream. Using a sharp knife and a template, cut out the shape of the telephone. Round off the edges and cut a shallow groove where the handle rests on the telephone. Place on the cake board and brush with hot apricot glaze.

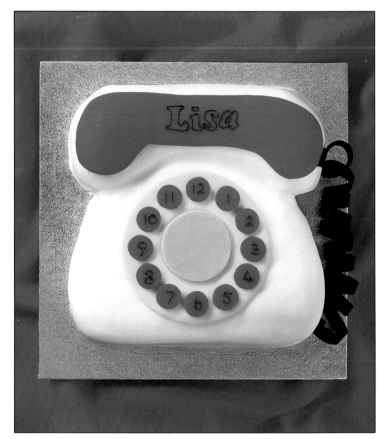

2 Cover the cake with marzipan then white fondant. Color half the remaining fondant yellow, roll out and cut a 3 in circle for the dial. Color a small piece blue and the rest of the fondant red and cut out 12 small red disks for the numbers (with a piping tube) and a 2 in blue disk for the center. Stick into place with a little water.

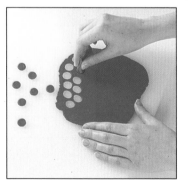

3 Twist the liquorice around to curl it for the cord, stick the ends to the fondant and secure with royal icing. Color the royal icing black and pipe numbers and the name of child on the telephone.

Box of Chocolates

This sophisticated looking cake is perfect for a very grown-up birthday and will delight chocolate lovers young and old. Substitute 1½ oz flour for cocoa to make a chocolate sponge.

INGREDIENTS
6 in square cake
¼ cup butter cream
apricot glaze
2¼ cups marzipan
1½ cups red fondant
¾ cup white fondant
food coloring: red
chocolates

EQUIPMENT
8 in square cake board
small paper candy cups
1½ yards × 1½ in wide gold and red
   ribbon

apricot glaze

chocolates

marzipan

fondant

1 Split and fill the cake with a little butter cream. With a sharp knife, cut a shallow square from the top of the cake, leaving a ½ in border around the edge. Place on the cake board and brush with hot apricot glaze. Cover with a layer of marzipan.

2 Roll out the white fondant and cut into a 7 in square. Lay it in the hollow dip and trim off the excess. Roll out the red fondant and cover the sides.

3 Put the chocolates into paper cases and arrange in the box. Tie the ribbon around the sides and tie a big bow.

Rosette Cake

This lovely cake is actually very quick to decorate. If the icing becomes too soft, put it in the fridge to firm up. If you make a mistake, then you can always try again until you get a good finish.

INGREDIENTS
8 in square cake
2¼ cups butter cream
apricot glaze
food coloring: dark red
crystallized violets

EQUIPMENT
10 in square cake board
cake comb
no. 8 star tube
candles

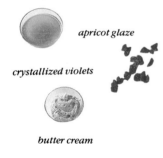

apricot glaze

crystallized violets

butter cream

1 Split and fill the cake with a little butter cream. Place in the center of the cake board and brush with hot apricot glaze. Color the remaining butter cream dark pink. Spread the top and sides with butter cream.

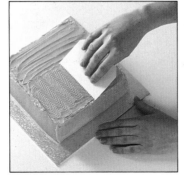

2 Using the cake comb; hold it against the cake and move it from side to side across the top to make waves. Hold the comb against the side of the cake, resting the flat edge on the board, draw along to give straight ridges down each side.

3 Put the rest of the butter cream into a piping bag fitted with a star tube. Mark a 6 in circle on the top of the cake and pipe stars around it and around the base of the cake. Place the candles and flowers in the corners.

Gift-wrapped Package

If you do not have a tiny flower cutter for the design on the 'wrapping paper' then press a small decorative button into the fondant while still soft to create a pattern.

INGREDIENTS
6 in square cake
¼ cup butter cream
apricot glaze
3 cups marzipan
2¼ cups pale lemon yellow fondant
food colorings: yellow, red and green
2 tbsp royal icing

EQUIPMENT
8 in square cake board
small flower cutter (optional)

apricot glaze

fondant

1 Split and fill the cake with butter cream. Place on the cake board and brush with hot apricot glaze. Cover with half the marzipan then yellow fondant and mark the paper with a small flower cutter. Divide the remaining marzipan in half, color one half pink and the other pale green. Roll out the pink marzipan and cut into four 1 × 7 in strips. Roll out the green marzipan and cut into four ½ in strips the same length. Center the green strips on top of the pink strips and stick onto the cake with a little water. Cut two 2 in strips from each color and cut a V from the ends to form the ends of the ribbon. Stick in place and leave to dry overnight.

2 Cut the rest of the green into 1 × 3 in lengths and the pink into ½ × 3 in lengths. Center the pink on top of the green, fold in half, stick ends together and slip over the handle of a wooden spoon, dusted with cornstarch. Leave to dry overnight. Cut the ends in V shapes to fit neatly together on the cake. Cut a piece for the join in the center, and fold in half with the join at the bottom.

3 Carefully remove the bows from the wooden spoon and stick in position with royal icing.

Baby's First Cake

The fondant dries quickly so have the cake marked out in sections before you attempt to make the swags around the sides.

INGREDIENTS
8 in round cake
¾ cup butter cream
apricot glaze
3 cups marzipan
3 cups pale yellow fondant
¾ cup white fondant
¾ cup royal icing
food colorings: yellow and blue
pink dusting powder

EQUIPMENT
10 in round cake board
no. 1 piping tube
6 small blue bows

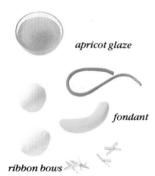

apricot glaze

fondant

ribbon bows

I Split and fill the cake with butter cream. Place on the board and brush with hot apricot glaze. Cover with a thin layer of marzipan then pale yellow fondant, extending it over the board. Measure the circumference of the cake with a piece of string and cut a strip of paper of the same length and depth as the cake. Fold the paper into six sections, mark with a deep scallop and cut in the top edge. Use to mark the swags on the side of the cake with a sharp needle.

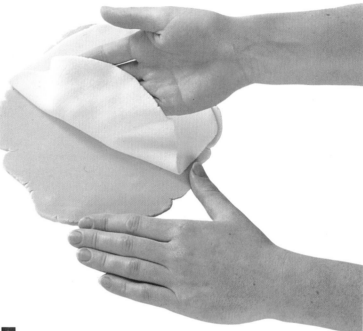

2 Color 1 tbsp of white fondant pale blue and roll out thinly. Wet a paint brush with water, remove excess on paper towelling and brush lightly over the fondant. Roll out thinly the same quantity of white fondant, lay this on top and press together. Roll out together to an 8 in square.

COOK'S TIP
The powder tints must be mixed with a drop of vodka or gin as they evaporate more quickly than water and do not have a chance to dissolve the delicate icing.

3 Cut ¼ in strips, carefully twist each one, moisten the swag marks with water and drape each barley twist into place, pressing lightly to stick to the cake.

4 Using a template, mark the knitting in the center of the cake. Cut out the sweater from white fondant and stick into place with a little water.

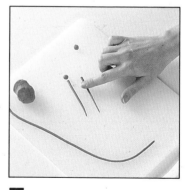

5 Roll a little fondant into a ball and color a small amount blue. Roll into two tapering 3 in long needles with a small ball for the end. Dry overnight.

6 Stick the needles and ball in position and with royal icing and a no. 1 tube, pipe knitting and stitches over needles and a trail of wool to the ball. Pipe over the ball with wool. Pipe a border around the base of the cake. Stick small bows around the edge of the cake with a little royal icing and carefully brush the knitting with powder tints.

Sweetheart

The heart-shaped run-outs can be made a week before the cake is made to ensure that they are completely dry. Once these are made, the cake can be quickly decorated.

INGREDIENTS
8 in round cake
¾ cup butter cream
apricot glaze
3 cups marzipan
4½ cups pink fondant
food coloring: red
¾ cup royal icing

EQUIPMENT
10 in round cake board
no. 1 writing tube
1¾ yards × 1 in ribbon wide
candles

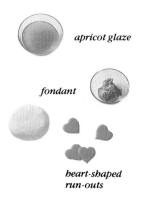

apricot glaze

fondant

*heart-shaped
run-outs*

1 Split and fill the cake with butter cream. Place on the cake board and brush with hot apricot glaze. Cover with a layer of marzipan then a layer of pink fondant, large enough to cover the cake and the board. Smooth the surface and trim off the excess. Mark the edge with the decorative handle of a spoon.

2 Using a template, make the heart-shaped run-outs. Leave to dry for at least 48 hours.

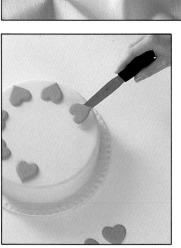

3 Arrange the hearts on top of the cake and place the candles in the center. Tie the ribbon round the cake.

Number 10 Cake

This is a very simple cake to decorate. If you cannot master the shell edge, then pipe stars around the edges to neaten.

INGREDIENTS
8 in round cake
6 in round cake
3 cups butter cream
apricot glaze
sugar strands
food coloring: red

EQUIPMENT
10 in round cake board
wooden toothpick
plastic number 10 cake decoration
no. 7 shell tube
no. 7 star tube
candles

apricot glaze

butter cream

sugar strands

1 Split and fill both cakes with a little butter cream. Brush the sides with hot apricot glaze. When cold, spread a layer of butter cream on the sides then roll in sugar strands to cover.

2 Color the rest of the icing pink, spread over the tops of each cake. Place the small cake on top of the large cake. Using a toothpick, make a pattern in the icing on top of the cake.

3 Use the remaining pink icing to pipe around the base of the cakes and around the edge. Stick the number 10 decoration in the center of the top tier and two candles on either side. Arrange the other candles evenly around the bottom cake.

Cloth Cake

Bright red fondant is quite difficult to achieve at home because so much color paste is needed. To save time, you can purchase it from specialist shops. The tiny bows can be bought at department stores and cake shops.

INGREDIENTS
8 in round cake
¾ cup butter cream
apricot glaze
3 cups marzipan
3 cups red fondant
1½ cups white fondant
¾ cup royal icing
food coloring: red

EQUIPMENT
10 in round cake board
no. 1 piping tube
no. 0 plain tube
no. 2 plain tube
wooden toothpicks
8 red ribbon bows
spoon with decorative handle

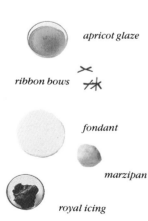

apricot glaze

ribbon bows

fondant

marzipan

royal icing

1 Split and fill the cake with butter cream. Place on the board and brush with hot apricot glaze. Cover with a layer of marzipan then red fondant, extending it over the board. Brush the lower edge of the cake with a thin band of water. Roll the rest of the red fondant into a thin rope long enough to go round the cake. Lay neatly around the base of the cake and cut off the excess. Mark with the decorative handle of a spoon. Leave to dry overnight.

4 Mark the child's name in the center and pipe with a no. 0 tube.

2 Roll out the white fondant to a 10 in circle and trim neatly. Lay this icing over the cake and quickly drape 'cloth' over wooden toothpicks at eight equal positions around the cake.

3 Mark a 4 in circle in the center of the cake. Using a template of the small flower design, transfer to the cake with a needle. Press a fine knitting needle or skewer into the fondant to make the flowers. The red color should show through – do not press quite so deeply for the stems and leaves.

5 Stick on the bows with a dab of royal icing. With a no. 2 plain tube and white royal icing pipe around the circle in the center. With a no. 1 plain tube, pipe small dots around the edge of the cloth to finish.

TEMPLATES

*T*he following templates, unless otherwise specified, are shown here at half their actual size. Scale up to the size required on tracing paper before using.

pinball machine

computer game

kite

92

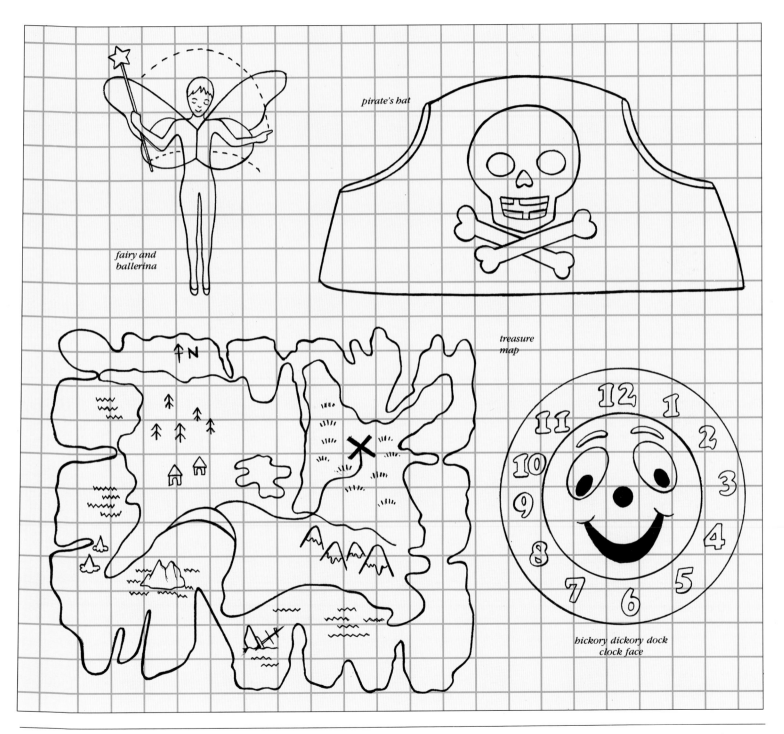

fairy and
ballerina

pirate's hat

treasure
map

hickory dickory dock
clock face

monkey

balloons

clown face

dart board

template
teddy

music sheet

cloth cake motif
(actual size)

ABCDEFGHI
JKLMNOPQRS
TUVWXYZ

abcdefghijklmn 1234567890
opqrstuvwxyz

INDEX

A
Apricot glaze, 11
Army tank, 76

B
Baby's first cake, 86
Ballerina, 80
Balloons, 66
Basic recipes, 12
Basic sponge cake, 13
Bella bunny, 20
Box of chocolates, 83
Bumble bee, 32
Butter cream, 13

C

Cake boards, 8
Cake decorating, 10, 11
Cake
   lining, 11
   pans, 8
Camping tent, 50
Candle holders, 10
Candles, 10
Car, toy, 72
Cat in a basket, 18
Circus, 60
Cloth cake, 90
Clown face, 62
Coloring fondant, 15
Computer game, 56
Cutters, 10

D

Dart board, 54
Doll's house, 58
Drum, 61

E
Edible paste colors, 10
Electric beaters, 8
Equipment, 8

F
Fairy, 46
Fairy castle, 38
Fire engine, 74
Flower cutters, 11
Fondant
   coloring, 15
   gelatin, 15
   quick, 15
Frog prince, 44

G
Gelatin fondant icing, 15
Gift-wrapped package, 85

H
Hickory dickory dock, 28
Horse stencil, 33

I
Icing
   coloring fondant, 15
   gelatin fondant, 15
   quick fondant, 15
   royal, 14
Icing smoother, 8

J
Jack-in-the-box, 70

K
Kite, 64

M
Magic rabbit, 34
Marzipan, 14
Measuring spoons, 8
Mice, sugar, 11
Mixing bowls, 8
Monkey, 21
Mouse in bed, 22

N
Noah's Ark, 30
Novelties and toys, 11
Number 10 cake, 89
Number 6 cake, 77

P
Paintbrushes, 8
Palette knives, 8
Party teddy, 27
Pastry brush, 8
Pastry cutters, 8
Pinball machine, 48
Pink monkey, 21
Piping
   bag, using, 16
   metal tubes, 11
   run-outs, 17
   waxed paper bag, making, 16

Pirate's hat, 41
Plastic chopping board, 8
Plastic scrapers, 8
Plastic train set, 11
Powder blossom tints, 11

Q
Quantities, 12
Quick fondant icing, 15

R

Racing track, 73
Ribbon bows, 11
Rolling pin, 8
Rosette cake, 84
Royal crown, 42
Royal icing, 14
Run-outs, 17

S

Sable paintbrushes, 8
Sailing boat, 52
Sand castle, 53
Serrated knives, 8
Sheet of music, 57
Sieves, 8
Space ship, 78
Spider's web, 24
Sponge cake, basic, 13
Sugar mice, 11
Sweetheart, 88

T

Teddy, party, 27
Teddy's birthday, 26
Telephone, toy, 82
Templates, 17
Toothpicks, 8
Toy car, 72
Toy telephone, 82
Treasure chest, 36
Treasure map, 40
Turntable, 8

W
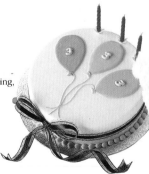
Wading pool, 67
Waxed paper piping bag, making,
   16
Weighing scales, 8
Wooden cocktail sticks, 8
Wooden spoons, 8